Original title:
Where the Green Lives

Copyright © 2025 Creative Arts Management OÜ
All rights reserved.

Author: Nathaniel Blackwood
ISBN HARDBACK: 978-1-80581-856-4
ISBN PAPERBACK: 978-1-80581-383-5
ISBN EBOOK: 978-1-80581-856-4

Secrets Held in Sylvan Folds

In the woods, leaves are conspiring,
Squirrels plotting and cats admiring.
Branches twist into a dance,
Who knew trees had a wild romance?

A rabbit wears a fancy hat,
Declares itself a diplomat.
It hops with glee and shakes a paw,
A woodland meeting? An odd law!

The toadstools gossip, oh so spry,
About mushrooms that reach for the sky.
They giggle low, so very slick,
Whispering jokes about the chick!

Nature's antics bring such glee,
Chatting creatures, wild and free.
With every rustle, a tale's unfolds,
Where secrets are held in sylvan folds.

Cradled by the Wilderness of Dreams

In the thicket, raccoons prance,
Wielding sticks and doing a dance.
They jive with owls in the night,
Creatures conspiring till daylight.

A bear sports shades, feeling so cool,
While a deer plays the fool at school.
They giggle at moons that blush and shine,
Birthday parties for trees, how divine!

Frogs in tuxedos croak a tune,
Underneath a quirky moon.
Their voices echo, a grand debut,
Who knew grads could be this few?

With laughter sprinkled on ferny beds,
Life's a sketch, where whimsy spreads.
Cradled in dreams, they seem to scheme,
A wild world, a funny theme!

Life's Forgiving Embrace

In a world where grass has jokes,
And trees giggle with their spokes,
A squirrel stashes nuts with glee,
While rabbits plan their next big spree.

The flowers wear their brightest hats,
As lazy bumblebees play chats,
Underneath the laughing sky,
A dance of life is always nigh.

Even worms do wiggly prance,
While ants engage in their fine dance,
The soil whispers secrets bold,
In this realm, all tales are told.

With every laugh and gentle sway,
The sun reminds us, come what may,
Life's quirks bring the best of cheer,
In this place, no room for fear.

Threads of Growth in Starlit Nights

Under stars, there's mischief afoot,
Moonlit plants trade their finest fruit,
A cactus jests, 'I'm the prickly king!',
While night blooms giggle at everything.

Crickets play their late-night tune,
As fireflies flirt with the moon,
In this garden of humorous sights,
Growth dances under starlit nights.

Snapdragons snap with a witty smile,
While overgrown weeds play the style,
Frogs leap with a joyful croak,
In this night, the laughter's no joke.

With every twinkle in the skies,
The grass whispers, 'What a surprise!'
Life unfolds in wacky ways,
In the glow of these silly days.

The Garden's Silent Revelations

With whispers soft, the garden sighs,
Insects giggle, while sunflowers rise,
Beneath the leaves, secrets abound,
In silence, funny truths are found.

A gnome winks with a mischievous cheer,
While veggies hold a secret seer,
Potatoes plot beneath the ground,
With every planting, humor's found.

The tomatoes blush with a funny bash,
While carrots dance in a vibrant flash,
All life here plays a jesting part,
In this plot, laughter's an art.

In every corner, magic's loose,
Life reveals its comic juice,
A place where chuckles intertwine,
In the garden's silly design.

Petals in the Breeze

Petals prance on winds so light,
As bees declare it's party night,
With pollen jokes that fill the air,
The flowers chuckle, 'Life's so rare!'

A dandelion's playful puff,
Spreads seeds of laughter, just enough,
While butterflies, with multi-hues,
Flit around, sharing funny views.

The grass tickles our toes with glee,
As plants join in on the jubilee,
Nature's joy, a vibrant spree,
In every leaf, a grin to see.

With sunshine painting laughs on leaves,
The breeze takes giggles, never grieves,
In a world where humor's free,
Petals dance in sweet harmony.

Reveries in the Thicket

Among the bushes, a squirrel pranced,
Chasing shadows, it almost danced.
A rabbit grinned, gave him a wink,
"Stop chewing grass, don't you ever think?"

A wise old owl in a tree so tall,
Said, "Life's a game, come join the ball!"
The hedgehogs chuckled, rolling about,
"Oh look, it's the nutty, forgetful scout!"

The breeze tickled leaves, made them sway,
"Dance with us!" the ferns seemed to say.
But a lazy frog just croaked and sighed,
"Does it pay off?" he muttered, fried.

Arbor Letters to the Moon

Dear Moon, in the sky so bright,
Do you see the trees bickering at night?
They argue over who's tallest of all,
While the stars just giggle, enjoying the sprawl.

The oaks claim wisdom, the birches are spry,
But the pines puff up, saying, "We touch the sky!"
Yet below, the daisies roll in the grass,
"Who cares about tall? We're the ones with class!"

So dear Moon, listen close to their shouts,
As the zany flora becomes the talk of the routes.
Each branch and leaf has stories to share,
Sign them 'Whacky' with love and flare.

Whirling through Spirals of Green

Round and round, the leaves take flight,
Spinning with joy, a carefree sight.
A rabbit hopped into the fray,
"Can we dance? Let's frolic and play!"

The daisies cheer, their petals aflutter,
While busy ants form a line, in their clutter.
"Step aside, you leafy crew,
We've got work to do, oh what a zoo!"

Yet the party thrived, amidst work and fun,
Even the slugs slid in with the pun.
So twirl and whirl, let laughter ring,
In this merry chaos, where creatures cling.

The Blossom's Promise

In the garden, blossoms tease,
"Bet you can't catch us dancing in the breeze!"
The bees buzzed in, with mischief unheard,
"Don't worry, we'll catch you, just wait for the word!"

A sunflower laughed, swaying so tall,
"Just stick to the rhythm, you won't fall!"
But a bold little bud got tipsy with glee,
"Twirling's my mission, come dance with me!"

Yet the raindrops dropped, splashing with cheer,
"Let's do a conga right over here!"
So petals swirled in a vibrant parade,
A promise of fun that never would fade.

Threads of Verdancy in Twilight's Quiet

In the hush of dusk, the grass creeps,
It tickles toes, and makes me squeal,
The daisies chatter, the whispers seep,
As nature's jesters spin a wheel.

Hedgehogs parade in snazzy hats,
While turtles race on wheels of cheese,
A squirrel debates with acorn rats,
Oh, life's a whirling, leafy breeze!

Bumblebees jig in hilarious flaps,
The sunflowers giggle, heads so high,
The crickets sing in rhythmic claps,
While fireflies wink and pass us by.

So, toss your woes in the leafy stew,
And join the revels, don't delay,
For in this leafy, vibrant view,
Each chuckle echoes the light of play.

Embracing the Soul of Each Leaf

Every leaf holds a joke anew,
With rustling laughs beneath the tree,
Mice wear coats of morning dew,
As frogs compose their symphony.

A dandelion sips from the rain,
Tickling the toad, causing a grin,
While ants in tuxedos complain,
That grasshoppers always win.

With wind as the jester, trees sway tight,
Spinning tales of whimsy untold,
And shadows dance in the soft moonlight,
As laughter breaks, forever bold.

So come, gather 'round this leafy play,
Embrace the quirks of each green friend,
For in this sanctuary's bright array,
The fun and folly never end!

The Lustrous Veins of Earth

Beneath the soil, the creatures sing,
With roots that tickle, a band of cheer,
Worms in tuxes do their thing,
And moles wear shades, their vision clear.

The daisies scheme a garden prom,
While carrots boast of being tall,
As roses debate a floral mom,
The earth laughs, as it spins in thrall.

Pebbles giggle, bouncing along,
Saying hello to the sprouting seeds,
With nature's rhythm, a quirky song,
Where every sprout towards laughter leads.

In this fertile ground, joy ignites,
An orchestra of silly and sweet,
Where glee takes root, and fun delights,
In every corner, life's heartbeat.

Poetry Written by the Wind

Whispers carried on breezy wings,
Scribbled notes across open fields,
The trees recite what the wind brings,
In playful rhymes, their laughter yields.

Clouds wear hats crafted from fluff,
Tickling the tops of pines in jest,
And every gust says, 'Life is tough,'
As squirrels conspire, never at rest.

Petals giggle, dance, and twirl,
While grasses sway in vibrant glee,
In the circus of life, we all whirl,
As nature writes its ode, carefree.

So let your troubles drift away,
On the breeze of mirth-filled delight,
Join the fun in this wild ballet,
As wind spins poetry, pure and bright.

Symphony Among the Greenery

In the forest, birds do sing,
Squirrels dance and madly swing.
Frogs with tuckered-out ballet,
Argue who can leap the way.

Trees wear hats of leafy cheer,
While raccoons sneak up with a beer.
The wind whips past in playful rhyme,
Tickling the flowers, what a time!

Beneath the bushes, secrets lie,
A stash of snacks from passersby.
A hedgehog juggles acorns round,
As laughter echoes through the ground.

Oh, the joy this green can bring,
With nature's oddness, we all sing!
Life's absurdity found in bloom,
Amidst the chaos, there's room!

The Breath of Rolling Hills

Up the hill, the rabbits race,
Winning's just a furry face.
Gophers pop up to say hi,
While daisies wave as they trot by.

The grass whispers its secret tale,
Of how it dreams to be a whale.
Its green ambition fuels a grin,
As butterflies fly with a spin.

Picnickers pack food with delight,
Ants host feasts—it's quite the sight.
As sandwiches vanish with a crunch,
Critters marvel at lunch's munch.

Rolling hills, so full of jest,
Here, nature plays and we all jest.
With laughter echoing in the breeze,
Life's wonders bring us to our knees!

Shadows of the Ancient Grove

In the grove where shadows fall,
Old trees giggle, that's their call.
Mushrooms wear a polka dot,
Dancing feet that twist a lot.

Owls hoot riddles in the night,
While moonbeams laugh at their delight.
Stick bugs fashion hats of twigs,
Hosting parties for the jigs.

Beneath the boughs, a treasure's found,
A pickle jar turned upside down.
Fireflies twinkle, join the fun,
A sparkly dance 'til day is done.

Ancient trees, the jokers wise,
Hold secrets, laughter in disguise.
In their shadows, we find relief,
Nature's jesters, ever brief!

A Tapestry of Life Unfolds

Colors splash where critters roam,
A patchwork quilt that feels like home.
Bumblebees conduct a buzz,
To rhythms that stir and fuzz.

Frolicsome foxes wear their flair,
With tails like feathers, they take air.
A dancing hedgehog steals the show,
Performing spins while stealing flow.

Grasshoppers leap, holding their breath,
In a contest of life and death.
The ladybugs sport tiny crowns,
As all around them the party drowns.

In this tapestry, joy unfolds,
Nature's antics, forever bold.
With every twist and turn, we see,
Life's a quilt of hilarious glee!

The Dance of Blossom and Breeze

In the meadow, flowers shake,
As the wind gives them a wake.
Daisies laughing in a row,
In a giggling waltz, they glow.

Bumblebees in a buzzing spree,
Try to dance, then bump a tree.
Petals swirl like silly hats,
Squirrels laugh, oh, what of that!

Sunshine plays hide and seek,
With shadows that go *peek-a-boo* peak.
All the critters join the glee,
Even grumpy old Oak agrees!

So come along, don't be shy,
Join the fun beneath the sky.
In the garden's playful dose,
Nature's humor, it's all a dose!

Nature's Living Canvas

The brook sings in a giddy twist,
Painting ripples, it can't resist.
A canvas made of green and blue,
Every brushstroke, a wild debut.

Dandelions throw a party bold,
With wishes whispered, dreams unfold.
Nature's palette, bright and loud,
Colors jostle in a vibrant crowd.

A tree with limbs all out of place,
Wobbling like it's lost in space.
Mossy hats on rocks stand tall,
Nature's jest, it laughs at all.

So take a stroll, and have a peek,
At the artwork nature seeks to speak.
In every leaf and every smile,
There's a funny story waiting a while!

Cradle of the Foliage

In the emerald cradle, dreams are spun,
Where branches sway, and critters run.
A baby bird with a wobbly tune,
Tries to croon to the grumpy moon.

Leaves gossip on a rustling day,
Sharing secrets in a leafy ballet.
A raccoon juggles acorns wide,
While rabbits cheer from the hillside.

A turtle slow, with a shell that's bright,
Winks at the sun, what a funny sight!
The lizard chuckles, a sly little tease,
Claiming he's the fastest in the trees.

Every shadow holds a giggle, too,
In this cradle where laughter grew.
A whimsical world, so full of cheer,
In nature's lap, all's free and clear!

Green Horizons Unveiled

On the horizon, laughter calls,
As nature paints its happy walls.
Waves of grass in wild ballet,
Swaying like they're at a play.

The clouds gossip – what a sight,
As butterflies join in the flight.
A rabbit hops with sprightly grace,
Chasing sunbeams in a race.

In this space, joy's never far,
Every leaf is a shining star.
Even rocks have a story to tell,
In this funny realm where all is well.

Come dance along this playful line,
Where all things twinkle and brightly shine.
In the heart of green, find a grin,
Where laughter grows and life begins!

Beneath the Arch of Organic Hearts

Beneath shady trees so spry,
Squirrels plotting all nearby,
They stash their acorns with great flair,
While rabbits dance without a care.

The daisies chat with the old oak,
Sharing jokes, making us choke,
A bumblebee in striped attire,
Buzzes 'round like it's on fire.

In the realm of leafy green,
Laughter flows like a grand cuisine,
Each leaf's a joke, each root a pun,
Nature's comedy's just begun.

Under the sun, all frolic free,
With nature's joy, just you and me,
So bring your giggles, join the spree,
In this garden, we're all carefree.

A Vision Through the Floral Veil

Petals giggle, colors clash,
Hummingbirds zoom, oh what a flash,
In this bouquet, humor grows,
A vibrant realm where fun overflows.

The roses blush as daisies tease,
While butterflies float with elegant ease,
They whisper secrets in the breeze,
Nature's antics put hearts at ease.

With every flower's glowing face,
They compete in a floral race,
Petal by petal, leaf by leaf,
They laugh at our human belief.

A vine swings low, a branch swings high,
While sunflowers grin at the sky,
So come and join this floral fate,
In this garden, we celebrate.

Chronicles from the Arboreal Depths

In the woods where shadows play,
Trees can gossip all day,
A squirrel narrates wild tales,
While lowly mushrooms brew their ales.

With acorns dropped like witty jabs,
The owls hoot while the fox grabs,
Tales of valor, tales of fright,
Echo through the woods at night.

Each creature bears a funny quirk,
The porcupine's dance, it does jerk,
Grasshoppers leap in hilarious coulds,
As if conducting nature's moods.

So take a step through leafy halls,
Where laughter rises, and nature calls,
In the depths of timber and bark,
Find the fun, ignite the spark.

Untamed Pathways of the Enchanted

Through winding paths where critters roam,
A frog complains it lost its home,
While foxes dart with a cheeky flair,
Mice in top hats toast the air.

The trees wear masks of sneaky grace,
Hiding secrets, just in place,
Each rustling leaf a whisper plays,
Telling stories of wild days.

Dandelions blow their seeds like dreams,
While snails plot to win their teams,
A turtle fast in his own way,
Declares it's time for his buffet.

So wander forth, discover glee,
In wild angles, let yourself be free,
In this enchanted, playful flight,
The fun of nature shines so bright.

The Lush Tapestry Unfolds

In the garden, plants conspire,
Leaves whisper secrets, never tire.
The squirrel sings with great delight,
Chasing shadows, what a sight!

The daisies dance in silly rows,
Rabbits hop with funny woes.
A butterfly steals a slice of cake,
And all the flowers start to shake!

A vine sticks out its leafy tongue,
While crickets chirp their silly song.
The sun tickles every petal,
As frogs join in—a jumping medal!

This tapestry of laughter spun,
Where plants and beasts all have their fun.
In the greenery, joy abounds,
Petal pals in giggles, laughter sounds!

Canopies of Calm Confession

Under trees with gossiping leaves,
A raccoon snickers, oh, how he heaves!
The owls hoot as if to tease,
While branches sway in playful breeze.

A sloth hangs upside down, so sly,
Winking at birds that zoom on by.
"It's nap time!" the lazy limbs doth shout,
As squirrels dart about with joyous clout.

The moss shares stories, deep and grand,
Of the antics of a wandering band.
A beetle lists out all his plans,
To become the greatest upstart, no ifs, ands, or cans!

In this green house of charming jest,
Every creature feels quite blessed.
With laughter wrapped in the leafy sun,
Nature's humor is never done!

Green Beyond the Horizon

The hills are ticked with emerald dreams,
As rabbits plot and plot in teams.
A turtle shouts from his slow parade,
"Let's have a race, but my way's delayed!"

Cactus stands tall, all prickly and proud,
Sassier than clouds in a fluffy shroud.
"Watch out!" warns the thyme in a nosey tone,
As bees buzz by like they own the zone.

A frog tells jokes that only he knows,
While aloe whispers tips for growing toes.
"Stretch up high," says the sunflower tall,
As daisies giggle, "We'll help you all!"

Their laughter spills over the green expanse,
A motley crew, forever in dance.
In plush places where silliness thrives,
Each leaf shares secrets, oh, how it jives!

Songs of the Flourishing Earth

Tune your ears to the rustling grass,
As worms take turns to sing and pass.
The wind flirts with dandelions' fluff,
Telling them jokes—oh, it's quite enough!

Ladybugs tap dance on a leaf,
While ants hold meetings, sharing belief.
"Don't step here!" a thistle exclaims,
Pointing to paths with silly claims.

A parrot squawks a raucous tune,
As flowers sway beneath the moon.
"Let's throw a bash!" a fox suggests,
Where tree trunks gather for their quests.

Songs of laughter ring out so clear,
With each note, the green draws near.
In this world where both giggles and gigants reign,
Nature joyously hits the refrain!

The Heart of Lush Existence

In backyards, plants laugh and sway,
The daisies gossip, come what may.
The grass tickles toes in a playful game,
While trees throw shade, never feeling lame.

Worms wear hats, they twirl and dance,
Squirrels hold parties, a grand chance!
Rabbits in tuxedos, what a sight,
Under moonlit skies, such pure delight.

The flowers sing tunes, oh what a show,
And ants march by, in neat little row.
Nature's committee, with laughter and cheer,
A jolly assembly, always near.

Blades of grass create a fuzzy cheer,
As garden gnomes sip on lemonade, dear.
Life in green, a zany bash,
Where joy is common, and worries just splash.

Echoes of Nature's Symphony

Crickets croon to the moonlight's beam,
While frogs compose their wetland dream.
Birds set the tempo, what a sound,
In a symphony where joy is found.

Leaves clap hands on a breezy day,
As branches move in a grand ballet.
A squirrel in tights hits a grand high note,
As honeybees hum from flower to boat.

The wind plays tricks with a feathered tease,
Tickling the trees with a gentle breeze.
Nature's orchestra never gets tired,
With laughter and mischief, it's all inspired.

A worm on stage takes a bold little bow,
While flowers burst into giggles, wow!
In this concert of nature's jest,
Every creature joins in, feeling blessed.

In the Shade of Emerald Dreams

Under leafy canopies, we meet,
With sunshine dancing, oh what a treat.
Mushrooms wear hats, a funny sight,
As shadows play tricks in soft twilight.

Frogs leap high like they own the place,
While bumblebees buzz with a vibrant grace.
The grasshoppers chirp, "Join us, don't flee!"
A party of critters for you and for me.

Dandelions blow wishes, so bright and bold,
With hopes and dreams that never grow old.
In this world of green, we giggle and play,
As nature spins tales in a whimsical way.

The twigs whisper jokes that the leaves all know,
As we lounge beneath with a breezy flow.
Together we share in this joyous scene,
In the shade of laughter, where bliss is routine.

A Tapestry of Leaf and Light

Nature weaves colors with laughter and cheer,
As bright blooms share gossip, loud and clear.
Petals wear crowns, all regal and grand,
In a kingdom of greenery, happy and planned.

Twisting vines act like jump ropes, you see,
As rabbits double-dutch in synchronized glee.
The sun paints the world with a playful hand,
Creating a canvas both bold and unplanned.

A raccoon in shades takes a prance so light,
While butterflies flit, oh what a delight!
Each day is a carnival, vibrant and free,
As nature holds court in its jubilant jubilee.

So join in the fun, leave your worries behind,
In this tapestry, laughter's entwined.
Life's a silly ride, full of glee,
In a realm where joy grows like a towering tree.

Serenity in Every Blade

In the park, the grass holds court,
Where squirrels plan their petty sport.
A picnic's nap turns into snore,
While ants throw food out the back door.

The flowers gossip, oh so bright,
They trade their petals, just for spite.
Laughter flutters with the breeze,
As bees wear tiny, buzz-filled tees.

A kick from a kid sends dirt a-flying,
While a dog nearby goes wildly trying.
The sun winks down with a cheeky grin,
Nature grumbles, "Guess I'm stuck in!"

Yet in this chaos, bliss finds a place,
With every laugh, a warm embrace.
In blades so green, the world's a stage,
Where even a worm can earn a wage.

Green Embrace of the Earth

Upon the hill, a goat does dance,
With moves that leave us in a trance.
The trees all chuckle, leafy and tall,
As mushrooms gossip, "He's having a ball!"

The flowers swear they've seen it all,
A squirrel's stunt that had him fall.
Grassy laughter fills the air,
As daisies nod, without a care.

A breeze that tickles every bloom,
Turns lazy critters into zoom!
Frogs croak tunes as if to say,
"Join the fun; don't waste the day!"

In every bumble, in every chirp,
Nature plays its goofy burp.
A patch so wild, so full of mirth,
This joyful jest — the heart of Earth!

Whispers of the Wild

In meadows wide, a shadow so small,
A rabbit's plan to rule it all.
With floppy ears, he breaks the sound,
While sneak-thief chipmunks race the ground.

The trees are gossips, whispering low,
"Told you, Tom, he'd steal that show."
Grass tickles toes, a playful tease,
As crickets chirp their evening breeze.

A butterfly shows off his flair,
While frogs in suits declare, "Beware!"
Lily pads bob with dapper style,
While dragonflies perform a while.

So listen close, when nature speaks,
In every giggle, joy peaks.
A wild embrace of colors and laws,
Nature's humor hides in every pause!

Portraits of Pastoral Harmony

Up in the fields, a cow strikes a pose,
With a grin that everyone knows.
Chickens boast a clucking choir,
As pigs roll mud in full-on attire.

The sun dips low, creating a stage,
Where every critter channels its rage.
A sheep in shades struts with pride,
While goats make mischief, they just can't hide.

The flowers wear hats, so floppy and bright,
While buzzing bees take off in flight.
"Baa-baa" sings the sheep with flair,
As frogs applaud from their comfy chair.

Each creature's dance is a sight to behold,
In this green world where stories unfold.
Nature's canvas, such a delight,
Makes every hour feel just right.

The Pulse of Flowered Valleys

In valleys bright where daisies cheer,
A bumblebee's dance brings us near.
He stumbles and shakes, a clumsy flight,
Is that a buzz or just delight?

Tall grasses laugh as the wind goes by,
They tickle the toes and wave hello, shy.
A flower's hat tips, quite the scandal,
Nature's gossip, we try to handle.

The sun spills gold on all that grows,
Even ants in their suits break out in a pose.
"Hey there, human, come join the fun!"
But we just can't, for we must run!

In fields alive with colors wild,
Nature's antics make us feel like a child.
With floppy hats and sneakers on,
We'll join the party until the dawn.

Roots of Resilience

Beneath the soil, a party bright,
Worms wear tuxedos, all dressed just right.
"Dig deeper!" they say with a wiggle of glee,
Roots throw confetti, oh what jubilee!

Trees shake their branches, perhaps they'll drop,
A ripe apple or two, become a tree hop!
Squirrels nearby shout, "What's the score?"
Racing to catch them, now that's a chore!

Each seed planted, with dreams that sprout,
Ode to persistence, there's never a drought.
"Keep your chin up!" the dandelions cheer,
"Life's a wild game, but we're all here!"

As twigs and leaves create a stage,
Grasshoppers leap, set to engage.
With laughter echoing through the glades,
Nature's circus, where joy invades.

In the Embrace of Nature's Palette

Brushstrokes in green, orange, and gold,
A canvas alive, with stories untold.
The sun and the clouds, they trade silly jests,
While rabbits play hopscotch in nature's best vests!

The pond, a mirror, shows a duck's wild hair,
Floating around with nary a care.
A turtle, a dancer, takes to the stage,
"Look at me, folks! I'm the star of the age!"

The petals gossip, in whispers and sighs,
"Did you see the frog? He just tried to fly!"
The painted butterflies flutter and tease,
In nature's embrace, we laugh with the breeze.

What hues can we find in this playful spree?
In the dance of the trees, oh, let's just be free!
With nature as artist, our hearts fill with cheer,
Embracing each moment, laugh, shout, and cheer!

Sanctuary of the Wild

In the wild, a sanctuary full of glee,
Koalas in pajamas, lounging in a tree.
They giggle and peek, plotting a prank,
While the lizards make bets on who's more crank!

Rabbits throw parties under the moon,
With carrots as snacks, they dance to a tune.
"Who can hop highest?" they challenge with pride,
Tomorrow's a race, for the fun's never dried!

The owls with their hats, sharp and so wise,
Share tales of the day, with wide-open eyes.
"Watch out for the fox," they joke and they hoot,
But he's busy with snacks, munching down his loot!

In this whimsical land, we smile and roar,
Nature's own carnival, we simply adore.
With friends all around, both furry and small,
In the wild's sanctuary, we love it all!

Surrendering to the Wilderness

In the forest, a bear wore a hat,
He danced with the squirrels, how about that?
Rabbits jumped high, with carrots on plate,
While a tortoise proclaimed, 'This party is great!'

A tree asked a shrub, 'Where's your big dreams?'
The shrub just giggled and burst at the seams.
'In this wild ruckus, we grow so carefree,
So pass me that salad, it's time for a spree!'

Foxes in sneakers, prancing about,
Debating on which route has the best clout.
While squirrels are plotting their nutty heist,
And a raccoon is thinking of snacks - how nice!'

Amidst all the laughs, the flowers just bloomed,
They whispered, 'In chaos, we find life resumed.'
With the trees as our friends, we all take a breath,
In the heart of the antics, we find fun in death.'

A Symphony of Leafy Whispers

In the glade, where the grass plays soft tunes,
A frog serenades under the light of the moons.
The branches, they giggle, while leaves sing along,
Oh, the laughter of flora, a wild, lively throng.

A hedgehog with glasses reads leaves like a book,
While foxes perform in their finest tux look.
They twirl and they spin, in a ballet of green,
And snicker at daisies, the stars of the scene.

A chorus of crickets joins in with a hum,
Their rhythm a tickle, and oh what a drum!
With whispers of petals, we waltz in delight,
In the concert of woodland, they dance till the night.

So come, be a part of this leafy affair,
With gossip from willow and cedar so rare.
Let the breezes embrace, let your worries all flee,
As nature performs, come play too, and be free!

Wandering Through Vocal Groves

I strolled past a willow, who waggled a leaf,
'Join me,' it winked, 'This party's a brief.'
The moss on the ground offered up a free snore,
A symphony of snoozes, who could ask for more?

Nuthatches debated the merits of song,
While ants choreographed, all organized throng.
A hedgehog declared, 'The pizza's just here!'
And all of the creatures broke out into cheer.

Branches would gossip, exchanging their tales,
Of sun, rain, and moonlight, like ancient old gales.
To wander through voices of soft rustling cheer,
Is a roller coaster ride; who knows what is near?

With laughter like bubbles, we played in the glen,
Got tangled in vines, like forgetful old men.
So take off your shoes, let the joy overflow,
In the warmth of the woods, let your worries let go.

The Sanctuary of Growing Things

In this haven of chaos, a pumpkin did grin,
He spoke to a squash, 'Let the fun times begin!'
With spinach on guard, and kale in the back,
They plotted a garden uprising, a snack attack!

Tomatoes were gossiping, sharing their juice,
A radish declared, 'We're the underground moose!'
With carrots in tutus, they pranced all around,
While beets joined the chorus with a boisterous sound.

An onion cried happy tears, why, who could know?
As flowers conspired with sunshine to grow.
Bubbles of laughter wafted up through the air,
In this sanctuary, we munch without care.

So come take a visit to this playful strange land,
Where veggies share secrets, all tasty and bland.
In the heart of the green, the fun does not cease,
Living wild and free, in the garden of peace!

In the Voting of Leaves

The leaves convene, a clever debate,
Deciding which branch is the best to date.
"I'm brighter!" one shouts, quite full of glee,
"No way, my dear, you're just full of me!"

While twigs act as judges in this silly brawl,
One acorn pops up, claiming he's small.
The squirrels are voting, cheering for fun,
But it seems the whole thing is just a pun.

Roots crack a smile as they wiggle around,
"Get with the program! We're earth's underground!"
The pine cones are playing, a game of charades,
Laughing together, in lovely cascades.

In the end, it's decided with chips and some bark,
Laughter erupts as they welcome the dark.
So who won this battle? It's anyone's guess,
Just another tall tale from the forest's address!

The Oasis Beneath a Thousand Stars

In the desert of life where the shadows are long,
A cactus wears shades, strumming a song.
The moonbeams giggle at this quirky sight,
As lizards do tango to the soft, silver light.

Grains of sand whisper jokes with the breeze,
"Hey, is that a mirage or just my cousin Lee?"
A lizard replies with a sound of a chuckle,
"Let's flip a coin, I'm tired of the shuffle!"

Palm trees sway like they're trying to dance,
While owls roll their eyes at the giraffe's prance.
A tumbleweed giggles, rolling on by,
"This party's so great, we should do it in July!"

Under a sky where the stars make a fuss,
The desert's alive, it's electric, it's us.
With laughter and light, it's a scene to recall,
An oasis of joy, where we giggle through all!

Shades of Meaning in Nature's Palette

In the colors of life, a paintbrush does play,
Grass green whispers secrets to the sun's golden ray.
A cherry tree giggles, its blossoms flutter,
"Hey there, Mr. Daisy, you smell like butter!"

The skies blush pink, wondering who's their beau,
Clouds dance a waltz, putting on quite the show.
A rainbow appears, wearing a mischievous grin,
"Guess what, my friends? I'm back with a spin!"

In the forest, the mushrooms all wear polka dots,
While squirrels hold court, discussing their plots.
"Do you think we can get the humans to see,
That we're the best thing, with air fresh like trees?"

Nature's palette laughs, o'er art it does prance,
In a world so absurd, who needs an advance?
Let's paint life in giggles and colors galore,
For every shade means there's laughter in store!

The Dance of Green Incantations

In the heart of the woods, the ferns start to sway,
They're casting some spells, come join the parade!
A lonesome old rock hums a base drum beat,
While mushrooms do disco, tapping their feet.

A wise old tree whispers sage advice,
"Don't take life too serious, just roll the dice!"
The beetles bring snacks, they've got quite the spread,
"Try these crunchy leaves, they'll dance in your head!"

Sunflowers chuckle, they're tall and quite proud,
"Don't shade us, buddy, we need a big crowd!"
The ants do a conga, as squirrels watch on,
"Hey, is that a tree, or just a giant prawn?"

As night starts to fall, they brighten the scene,
With fireflies twinkling, like jewels in between.
It's a whimsical dance, where laughter is found,
Each twist and each turn leaves us joyously bound!

The Poetry of Petals Unfurled

In the park, a squirrel's dance,
Twisting, turning, taking a chance,
With a nut in its paws, oh what a sight,
It seems to prepare for a nutty flight!

A flower shimmies, just like a star,
It swayed so hard, it nearly went far,
Bees buzz around, in a dizzy swoop,
Composing a tune like a wacky loop!

A daisy jokes with a laughing breeze,
"We're all just here to please and tease!"
The roses chuckle with petals' flair,
A garden party with scents to spare!

In this meadow, laughter grows tall,
Even weeds chuckle, they long for a ball,
With sunlight as punch and roots as the team,
Nature's comedy, a joyful dream!

Awakened by the Thrum of Life

A toad croaks loud, like a rock star's shout,
Frog legs flailing, there's no doubt,
Fly friends giggle, in a buzzing crew,
With every jump, it's a wild debut!

Grass blades stretch, in a yoga pose,
A worm peeks out, then quickly doze,
"Yoga is hard," the small bug sighs,
As the sun tickles with golden pies!

A rabbit hops to the rhythm of spring,
With floppy ears, it becomes a king,
Chasing shadows, in a silly race,
Home is where the fun finds its place!

Nature's laughter rings in clear waves,
Where creatures play like a bunch of knaves,
With zany antics, they swirl and twirl,
Through grass and blooms, they spin and whirl!

Rain-kissed Epiphanies

A raindrop splashes on a flower's hat,
"Hey there, buddy!" says the playful sprat,
Dancing on petals, they twirl with glee,
In this flood of joy, there's no fee!

Puddles beckon with a cheeky grin,
"Come splash around! Let the fun begin!"
Jumping about, we giggle and squeal,
The muddy "tuxedo" is simply ideal!

The trees wear crowns of water's pearls,
Swaying and bowing, in rain's light swirls,
Oh, the gossip of leaves fills the air,
Each drop a secret, a whimsical dare!

As laughter mixes with nature's tune,
Clouds giggle softly, like a big balloon,
The earth's a stage where we all can play,
In this rain-soaked dream, we find our way!

Beneath the Boughs of Solitude

Underneath branches, two ants discuss,
Planning a party, oh what a fuss,
With crumbs as confetti and dew as punch,
Their picnic will surely be a wild munch!

A snail creeps by, with a shell so grand,
"I'm the slowest racer in all the land!"
While worms giggle, ready to cheer,
"With speed like yours, we'll sell out next year!"

A whisper of leaves shares a silly tune,
Plotting a show with a luminous moon,
Critters in costumes, a hoot and a holler,
A bash beneath boughs, they'll dance and they'll baller!

The shadows stretch, as night whispers fun,
Neath the boughs, a revelry begun,
In every nook, a chuckle is spun,
In solitude's heart, the laughter's the sun!

Valleys of Flourishing Hues

In valleys deep where colors play,
The daisies dance, hip-hop all day.
They pull their petals, show their flair,
While bumblebees buzz, without a care.

The tulips giggle, red and bright,
They tell the daisies, "You're not quite right!"
Sunflowers laugh with their giant heads,
Debating who snoozes best in beds.

The grass thinks it's the tickling champ,
While worms below plot a little ramp.
A party forms with roots and stems,
Even fungi join, with their funky gems.

Oh, what a jolly, vibrant spree,
In valleys lush, wild and free.
A riot of laughs, a colorful scene,
Where nature's charm reigns evergreen!

The Secret Life of Sundrenched Groves

In groves where sunlight skips and hops,
The squirrels gossip, while the acorn drops.
Chatter and scamper, what a sight,
Their shadows dancing in the golden light.

The trees are gossip queens so grand,
With leafy crowns, they take a stand.
"Did you see the owl's new shades?"
They whisper softly under leafy cascades.

Rabbits waltz through tangles of blooms,
While ladybugs plan secret room zooms.
The mushrooms grin, they know all the jokes,
About chasing twigs and tickling folks.

Oh, in these groves, such antics abound,
Where giggles echo, and cheer is found.
Life unfolds in a vibrant play,
In dappled light, they party all day!

Dancing with the Forest Spirits

In a forest of laughter, under trees so tall,
Spirits twirl, and giggles enthrall.
They do the quickstep on mossy floors,
While owls keep time, tapping their scores.

The ferns sway gently, a dizzying dance,
Inviting the fox to take a chance.
"Step right up!" they call with glee,
As squirrels spin round, no need to flee.

A chorus of crickets strum their strings,
Encouraging all to join in the flings.
With shadows as partners, they prance 'round trees,
Where dandelion fluff stirs with the breeze.

This forest so merry, gleeful and bright,
Turns every moment into pure delight.
Join the waltz, let laughter unfurl,
In a twilight haven, where spirits twirl!

Meadow Muses Under Shimmering Skies

In meadows wide, where daisies cheer,
Muses gather, with joy so near.
They tiptoe on petals, sip morning dew,
Sharing silly tales of the skies so blue.

With butterflies painted in hues so bright,
They battle with bees in a playful fight.
"Who's the fastest?" they giggle and tease,
As clouds drift by on a whimsical breeze.

A frog in the pond croaks a croaky song,
While crickets join in, humming along.
"Life's but a jest," the wildflowers say,
"Let's laugh it up, chase worries away!"

Under shimmering skies, a canvas of cheer,
These meadow muses spread happiness here.
Every moment's a treasure, every smile a gift,
In this world of wonder, spirits uplift!

Lush Reverie

In a forest, I stumbled on a deer,
Wearing a hat and a grin ear to ear.
He told me a joke about a tall tree,
And offered me acorns for high tea.

The flowers all giggled, they played a tune,
While bugs did the cha-cha, beneath the moon.
A squirrel with glasses read books on a log,
I laughed so hard, I could hug a frog.

Whispering Meadows of Tomorrow

There's a goat who believes he can fly,
He jumps on the clouds, oh my, oh my!
The rabbits are keen on a dance-off today,
Bouncing and spinning, they sweep me away.

The daisies are planning a fancy parade,
With buttercups yelling, 'We're not afraid!'
The wind joins the fun, tickling each petal,
While butterflies ride on a grape soda kettle.

In the Heart of Verdant Fields

In fields so bright, the peasants convene,
With chickens on scooters, it's quite a scene.
A cow in sunglasses sings old rock 'n' roll,
While pigs do the worm, and the goats take a stroll.

The corn stalks have gossip, they whisper and chat,
Telling tales of the cat who ran off with a hat.
The sun beams down, it's a party galore,
While turnips do cartwheels, oh, what a chore!

Shades of Serenity

Under a tree, a raccoon plays chess,
With ants as his pawns, what a wise guess!
The breeze brings laughter from pools of bright dew,
As frogs in tuxedos serenade the view.

A ladybug juggles, while bees clap along,
Singing sweet harmony, it feels like a song.
With every soft rustle, the laughter will roam,
In this quirky green world, we're all right at home.

Emerald Echoes

In a land where vegans roam,
The broccoli sings a sweet ho-me!
Carrots dance in a vibrant hue,
As peas giggle, 'Come join us too!'

The lettuce wears a floppy hat,
While radishes joke, 'What's the matter?'
Cucumbers roll in the warm sun's glow,
And tomatoes blushing, 'Don't you know?'

Zucchini feels a bit out of place,
Says, 'All this humor's a hasty race!'
Herbs whisper puns from the ground,
As nature joins in with laughter round!

In this patch, where green things play,
Snack time comes with a punny display.
With every leaf a story to tell,
The emerald echoes ring out so well.

Forest Whispers Illuminate

In a forest full of silliness,
Trees tiptoe, causing great distress.
The squirrels chuckle, planning a heist,
Stealing acorns, oh what a feast!

Mushrooms wear caps that shine so bright,
Claiming they're the fashion elite tonight.
Fungi giggle, as they start to sway,
Saying, 'Join us for a spore-filled soirée!'

With critters holding a quirky debate,
Arguing if twigs really look great.
A raccoon claps in his best disguise,
Wearing leaves as a mask, much to our surprise!

Under the trees, laughter cascades,
While shadows dance in leafy parades.
Fun unravels through roots that conspire,
As nature's humor never tires!

Beneath the Canopy of Dreams

Beneath tall giants with leafy hats,
A spider cracks jokes that make us splat!
An owl hoots puns in the still of night,
While fireflies flicker with pure delight.

A raccoon roasts marshmallows in style,
Claiming to be the culinary guile.
The deer giggle, 'We could join in!'
With s'mores made from a fox's kin!

The grass whispers tales of a silly frog,
Who croaked out a song to a dancing dog.
A bashful turtle joins the fun,
Mimicking moves that have just begun!

In this dreamland of whimsy and cheer,
Every critter has a laugh to share here.
Under the canopy, let the joy stream,
For nature's rich humor's the wildest dream!

The Symphony of Leaf and Light

In a symphony of rustle and cheer,
Leaves tumble down like they've done a leer.
The branches sway to a funky beat,
While the sun plays tag with the grass at their feet.

Rabbits hop with a bouncy finesse,
Singing jingles in fashionable dress.
A parrot squawks 'Twist and shout!'
As flowers all dance, there's no doubt!

The breeze whistles tunes through the pirouetting trees,
Blowing away worries, like a playful tease.
With petals like trumpets, they join in the fun,
Creating a concert until day is done!

From dusk till dawn, the laughter ignites,
Nature is giddy with all its delights.
In this harmonious green delight,
Life sings sweetly through day and night.

Guardians of the Wooded Enclave

Squirrels in capes, they take flight,
Saving acorns by twilight.
With a giggle and a shout,
They chase the deer about.

Rabbits patrolling, fierce and stout,
Making sure all's safe, no doubt.
With helmets made of leaves and twine,
They guard the glens, oh what a line!

The owls wear glasses, read the news,
While the porcupines plan their snooze.
With giggles echoing from the trees,
Even the buzzards laugh with ease.

A meeting's called at the stump so wide,
To discuss just who's the best to ride.
Through vine and bark, they dream and scheme,
In this leafy land, it's a silly dream.

Between the Roots and the Rain

Dancing droplets, splashes grand,
Frogs burst forth, a joyful band.
With funky hops on slippery ground,
They croak a tune, a funny sound.

Under big hats made of moss,
Bumblebees buzz, they jostle across.
They laugh at blooms, so brightly bold,
Swapping tales of nectar gold.

Puddles reflect the sky's great cheer,
As gnomes gather, sharing a beer.
"Why'd the mushroom go to school?"
"To be a fungi! Now how's that for cool?"

Between the roots, they sing and play,
As frogs in tuxes strut all day.
The roots are home, a giggling maze,
In the rain's embrace, they spend their days.

The Pulse of Leafy Adventures

The forest pulses, alive with fun,
Chipmunks race 'til the day is done.
A squirrel on a skateboard zooms,
Over mushrooms in quiet rooms.

Hidden treasure in every nook,
A raccoon writes a silly book.
With pages torn in a prankster's fit,
Each laugh echoes, they can't quite quit.

A hedgehog juggles pinecones bright,
While fireflies dance, a glowing sight.
"Catch me if you can," the breeze will call,
As the trees sway and giggle, standing tall.

Each leaf tells tales of merry delight,
Gather 'round, let's party tonight!
In the hum of the woods, find laughter's art,
Where adventures bloom and never depart.

Serenity of the Wild Blooms

Petals flutter, a waltz so sweet,
Dancing bees on tiny feet.
With polka dots and colors rare,
They groove like they don't have a care.

A daisy told a rose one day,
"Why don't you join in our ballet?"
With laughter bright, they twirled around,
In flowers' joy, the peace they found.

Butterflies giggle in the breeze,
As they sip nectar with such ease.
"Why did the flower blush?" they tease,
"It saw the gardener's happy knees!"

In this meadow, humor is the balm,
A calming giggle, so blissfully calm.
Where petals sway and laughter blooms,
The world in bloom, where joy resumes.

Under the Canopy's Care

Squirrels dance with little flair,
While rabbits hop without a care.
A parrot's squawk, loud as a bell,
Sounds like a joke, can you tell?

Sunlight flickers like a tease,
Winding through branches, swaying with ease.
A mushroom's cap, a silly hat,
Toadstools chuckle, 'Ain't life fat?'

Bees buzz by with a jaunty tune,
Making honey 'neath the moon.
The flowers giggle, petals bright,
"Do we look good?" they ask in flight.

Here, nature's humor knows no bounds,
Even trees enjoy some rounds.
In this green world, laughter grows,
With every breeze, fun just flows.

The Lushness of Being.

Grass tickles toes with a playful greet,
While daisies giggle at my bare feet.
A snail slides by, all slimy and keen,
Saying, "I'm the fastest you've ever seen!"

Bees wear shades, looking oh-so-cool,
Rolling on petals, like it's a pool.
A frog croaks loudly, a song of cheer,
"Ribbit and roll, the party's here!"

Clouds shape-shift, resembling a snack,
"Is that a cupcake? I want to pack!"
A wiggly worm dons a tiny bow,
"Slimy and stylish, I steal the show!"

In this lush land, humor takes root,
Nature's charm in every shoot.
It's a world where joy runs wild,
Like a laughing, playful child.

Whispers of the Verdant Realm

Butterflies gossip in colors so bright,
They flutter about, a marvelous sight.
A hedgehog grumbles, "Why do I roll?"
"It's my lookout post; I'm on patrol!"

Leaves giggle softly at the passing breeze,
"Want a game of tag? Come, if you please!"
A turtle chuckles, slow and sincere,
"Life's not a race; let me make it clear!"

Singing streams waltz with rocks all around,
"Let's dance, dear friends, to nature's sound!"
Birds hold a concert, not missing a beat,
With worms in the crowd, they shuffle their feet.

In this secret place, laughter ignites,
A magical world where humor delights.
Every creature, a comedian at heart,
In the whispered green, we all play a part.

Beneath the Canopy's Embrace

Under the leaves, the secrets unfold,
Frogs in bow ties, feeling quite bold.
A squirrel takes selfies; it's quite a sight,
With acorns at hand, it's party tonight!

In the shade of the trees, laughter rings clear,
A raccoon with mischief and high-flying cheer.
Ants in a line think they're quite grand,
Skipping along, forming a band.

Vines swing like jump ropes in the breeze,
Nature's workout, designed to please.
A dandelion stands proud, oh so bright,
"Wish upon me, but first take a bite!"

Here in this jungle, joy takes the lead,
With every giggle, a moment to heed.
Life is a jest through nature's fine art,
In this lush playground, let laughter start!

Reflections in the Verdant Waters

Beneath the leaves, a splash so loud,
A frog jumps in, like a croaking crowd.
Ripples dance in a game of tag,
Fish wink at me; it's quite a brag.

Cattails swaying, a dance so grand,
A dragonfly lands, as if it planned.
I try to wave, but I just trip,
Falling in, with a spluttered quip.

A turtle glides by, with casual grace,
Winks his eye, "You're a funny case!"
I chuckle back, water's my friend,
In this bright world, laughter won't end.

Sunshine giggles, warming my soul,
As nature whispers its joyous roll.
Petals dancing, a floral parade,
I'm just the jester, in this green escapade.

Gentle Giants Whispering Secrets

Oh mighty trees with barks so wide,
Whispering stories that they can't hide.
Branching out, they seem to jest,
With acorns and sap, it's quite the fest!

Squirrels chatter, it's a comedy show,
Stashing their nuts, putting on a glow.
"Hey, pass that acorn!" they cheerfully shout,
As I laugh hard, trying to scout.

Beneath their shadows, I take a seat,
Trying to hide from a falling sheet.
A leaf plops down, right on my nose,
I guess that's nature's way to impose!

With every breeze that rustles around,
It's a playlist of giggles, a giggling sound.
In this forest of jesters, I'm just a guest,
Among gentle giants, I feel truly blessed.

The Hidden Heartbeat of Nature

In the hush of leaves, a heartbeat grows,
An ant on a mission, in quite the pose.
With tiny boots, he struts with style,
While I watch closely, with a goofy smile.

Bugs in a buzz, like a gossip spree,
Chatting about where they should be.
"Let's gather pollen, or just take a nap!"
Laughter erupts from this buzzing chap.

Grasshoppers leap, with comedic flair,
Bouncing along in the dappled air.
They sing a tune, so off-key but bright,
Nature's own band, in morning light.

With every beat, the woods come alive,
In this funny realm, we all connive.
I join the chorus, in my own little way,
In the heartbeat of life, I choose to stay.

In Praise of Fern and Moss

Oh fern so frilly, you tickle my toes,
With emerald fronds, in sweet repose.
You whisper softly as I stroll by,
"Join in my dance, don't be shy!"

Mossy carpets beneath my feet,
A squishy embrace, oh what a treat!
"Watch your step!" cries a nearby toad,
As I giggle, shifting my load.

Lichens join, with a wink and a grin,
They color the rocks with their charming spin.
"Don't get too comfy," the moss retorts,
"We're on a journey, through nature's courts!"

In this green kingdom, a merry crew,
With jests and laughter, and a fresh morning dew.
I bow to the ferns, and tip my hat,
For in this funny realm, I'm delighted like that!

Unveiling the Flora's Whisper

In the garden, gnomes take a break,
Sipping tea, for goodness' sake.
Roses giggle, tulips sway,
It's a plant party—come what may!

Worms in top hats dance around,
Crickets jump, they make quite a sound.
Ladybugs wear polka-dot shoes,
They argue over who will choose the blues!

Sunflowers sunbathe, 'Can't get enough!'
While daisies boast, 'This is real tough!'
In the shade, mushrooms regale,
Stories of ups and downs without fail!

So come, dear friends, and witness this show,
Where leaves can laugh and flowers glow.
It's nature's stage, playful and bright,
Join the whimsy; it feels just right!

Fidelity of the Toiling Roots

Oh, the trees gossip under the sun,
Squirrels jest, 'Let's have some fun!'
Moles dig deep with a secret plan,
While grasshoppers play their lively band.

The carrots complain, 'We're stuck in a plot!'
Roots intertwine, like a tangled knot.
'You think you're tough?' brags the celery sprout,
But all know the weeds are the ones to pout!

Beanstalks reach high, 'Look at me go!'
While pumpkins grumble, 'We're too slow!'
The wildflowers laugh, 'We can't be contained!'
Feeling free is the beauty unfeigned!

Each inch of soil holds tales untold,
Of laughter and joy in shades of gold.
So dig through the dirt and grab a good spoon,
For the roots are laughing, morning to noon!

Soliloquy of the Evergreen

Evergreens quip, 'We're the old and wise,'
'With needles that tickle and boughs that surprise!'
Pines tell stories of snowflakes they've met,
While firs throw shade without any regret!

Each morning, the leaves share a secret or two,
'Who's got the best view of the sky's bright blue?'
Maples chime in, all red and grand,
'Where else can you find such a colorful band?'

Branches reach out for a lively ballet,
Squirrels twirl, as if in a play.
Barking beetles knock on their bark,
Demanding respect, igniting a spark!

So listen close when they begin to muse,
Nature's comedians with nothing to lose.
Each whisper a giggle from above the ground,
Where the joyous songs of life abound!

The Green Horizon Vows

At dawn, the grass shakes off the dew,
Forgetfulness is a morning brew.
Flowers argue, 'I'm the brightest here!'
While daisies laugh in a hippy cheer!

Beneath the surface, roots have their fights,
Claiming turf at unwelcome nights.
Each leaf declares, 'I'll stretch and sway!'
As butterflies join this lively fray!

Caterpillars munch with a cheery grin,
Their most daring thought? 'Soon, we'll win!'
As sunflowers wink, saying, 'Watch us grow!'
In a world where antics steal the show!

It's a league of greens, under bright blue skies,
Nature's squad, filled with laughter and ties.
So skip through the fields, let joy be your creed,
For in this vibrant realm, there's always a need!

The Language of Blooming Souls

In fields of laughter, daisies dance,
Bees hold meetings, taking a chance.
Butterflies gossip, wearing their hues,
While grasshoppers leap in their Sunday shoes.

Trees tell stories, with a rustling breeze,
Squirrels debate about silly memories.
The daisies nod, so wise yet naive,
Playing hide and seek, they refuse to leave.

Picture this scene, a vibrant affair,
Mice in tuxedos, pretending to care.
Rabbits in bow ties, hopping along,
With this motley crew, you can't go wrong!

So join the festival, lift up your cheer,
Laughter and nature, perfectly clear.
In this lively world, let your spirit be free,
For in every flower, there's a joke, can't you see?

A Journey Through Tangled Shadows

In twisting paths, the shadows play,
Whispering secrets of a clumsy day.
The trees look down with a knowing grin,
A raccoon slips by, sporting a tin.

The cacti chuckle, in their prickly attire,
While worms dust off and crawl with desire.
A squirrel trips over, bumps its bushy tail,
Falling in style, without leaving a trail.

Moonbeams giggle, lighting the way,
As fireflies flash, it's a grand ballet.
The owls impersonate laughter so wise,
While crickets compose night symphonies that rise.

In shadows we wander, weaving through glee,
Finding the funny in every grand spree.
So let's spin and twirl in this odd little dance,
For every mishap can spark a new chance!

Nature's Heartbeats in Prayer

Leaves clap together, like hands in a choir,
Each rustle a cheer, never to tire.
The flowers look up, all wrinkled and bold,
Their petals shake secrets that never grow old.

The puddles reflect all the laughs up above,
While frogs croak their songs about mishaps in love.
A deer takes a bow, all graceful and spry,
As a butterfly flutters, "I swear I can fly!"

The clouds have a chat, drifting fluffy and light,
While squirrels host critiques on the cakes baked at night.
The winds carry whispers of giggles galore,
In this wild communion, who could ask for more?

So let's chant our joys, each heartbeat a prayer,
For in nature's embrace, we're all light as air.
With each laugh that erupts, see how hearts soar,
In this grand celebration, let worries be shore!

The Color of Tomorrow's Hopes

In splashes of colors, dreams take flight,
With rainbows playing, oh, what a sight!
The sunbeams chuckle, as they wrap up the day,
While daisies declare, "Join our bouquet!"

Each petal's a wish, fragile and bright,
Popping like popcorn, a marvelous sight.
The grass tickles toes in a playful embrace,
Encouraging giggles, that can't be replaced.

The clouds wear mustaches, quite silly indeed,
While ants march in line, following a lead.
Crickets give concerts, at dusk, with great flair,
As the moon takes a bow, in sequins so rare.

So color your dreams with laughter and cheer,
In this garden of hopes, there's nothing to fear.
For tomorrow awaits, with colors so grand,
In the whimsical life that love has planned!

Enchanted by Flora's Touch

In the garden, a gnome goes to dance,
Wearing a hat, with a wild, silly prance.
Flowers giggle, tickled by the breeze,
While the sun whispers secrets to the bees.

A squirrel pulls pranks on a lazy old cat,
Stealing its nap with a loud, raucous chat.
Beneath the daisies, they plot and they scheme,
Life's a joke, or at least a weird dream.

Butterflies flirt with the ladybug crew,
While the ants march with a plan to debut.
Dandelions laugh as they take to the air,
Sprinkling wishes like confetti everywhere.

In this realm of mirth, all worries are tossed,
With each quirky critter, no moment is lost.
So come join the fun where mischief's the king,
In this riotous garden, let laughter take wing.

The Lullabies of Springtime Meadows

Bouncing bunnies skipping, oh what a sight,
Singing to daisies, as day turns to night.
The grass tickles toes, it's a giggle fest,
In the meadow, the critters just never rest.

A hedgehog in shades croons a smooth little tune,
While fireflies flicker a light dance to the moon.
Chickens join in, clucking beats oh so sweet,
With frogs in the pond tapping out the offbeat.

The sunflowers sway like they've got a groove,
As the wind takes a turn, making all nature move.
Each petal a drum, each leaf a trumpet,
In this silly orchestra, no one can grump it.

And when the stars shine, the laughter won't cease,
For springtime's a party, a jubilant feast.
So join in the chorus, let your spirit be free,
In this joyful meadow, come dance with me!

In the Hands of Verdant Dreams

A frog in a bowtie regards the great sky,
Claiming he's destined to someday learn to fly.
With wings made of leaves and a helmet of moss,
He leaps with conviction, but hey—what a loss!

The flowers all chuckle, snickering bright,
As the frog crashes down in a cloud of delight.
"Don't worry," they say, "you'll soon find your flair,
Just steer clear of daisies, they don't like to share!"

An owl, oh so wise, with spectacles perched,
Reads from a book where the giggles are searched.
"Today in the garden, we'll brew up some fun,
With sprinkles of sunshine, and laughter's the sun!"

So gather your friends, let silliness reign,
In these verdant dreams, joy flows down like rain.
The frog drinks his tea, in a whimsical pose,
Making plans for next time, who knows where it goes?

Lush Horizons Broken Only by Sky

A deer with a bow wiggles its tail,
Dreaming of journeys, it'll set off to sail.
With fish for companions and clouds for a hat,
They plot an adventure—imagine that!

The birds all bring snacks, a feast in the air,
With seeds of all colors, floaty cheer everywhere.
A parrot tells jokes that make everyone roar,
While raccoons join in with a tap on the floor.

The trees hum a tune, swaying side to side,
As butterflies cheer with a soft, gleeful glide.
A panda rolls by, on a quest for some leaves,
Adding to the laughter, as nature believes.

So roam through this paradise, joyful and bold,
Where nature's the stage and the tales unfold.
Each critter's a star in this colorful show,
In lush horizons, let silliness grow!

www.ingramcontent.com/pod-product-compliance
Lightning Source LLC
Chambersburg PA
CBHW070315120526
44590CB00017B/2693